Sports Illustrated KIDS

FOOTBALL'S Most CONTROVERSIAL PLAYS YOU MAKE the CALL!

by Matt Chandler

CAPSTONE PRESS
a capstone imprint

Published by Capstone Press, an imprint of Capstone
1710 Roe Crest Drive, North Mankato, Minnesota 56003
capstonepub.com

Library of Congress Cataloging-in-Publication Data
is available on the Library of Congress website.
ISBN: 9798875257612 (hardcover)
ISBN: 9798875257568 (paperback)
ISBN: 9798875257575 (ebook PDF)

Summary: Take an in-depth look at three controversial football plays, review the ref's call, and make your own decision.

Editorial Credits
Editor: Christianne Jones; Designer: Tracy Davies; Media Researcher: Svetlana Zhurkin; Production Specialist: Whitney Shaefer

Image Credits
Associated Press: 4, 5, Al Messerschmidt, 14, Mark Humphrey, 12; Getty Images: Allen Kee, 13, Chris Graythen, 20, 21, Christian Petersen, 29 (left), Ethan Miller, 9, Jonathan Bachman, 18, Kevin C. Cox, 19, Otto Greule Jr, 26, Sam Greenwood, 11, Sam Hodde, 8, Stephen Maturen, 7, Winslow Townson, 10; Newscom: Cal Sport Media/George Holland, 24, Icon SMI/Ric Tapia, 25, 27, UPI Photo Service/Billy Suratt, 15; Shutterstock: inspired-fiona, 6, JoeSAPhotos, cover (bottom), Lana Sham, back cover, 17, 23, 28, 29 (right), Muhammad Muhdi (dotted background), cover (top) and throughout

Words in **BOLD** can be found in the glossary.

Printed and bound in China. PO 6459

TABLE OF CONTENTS

QUESTIONABLE CALL

It was the first day of 1978. The American Football Conference (AFC) Championship Game was underway in Denver. The Denver Broncos were up 7–3 in the second half against the Oakland Raiders. And the Broncos were driving for another touchdown. **Rookie** running back Rob Lytle took the handoff and dove toward the end zone—and lost the ball!

Raiders defensive end Mike McCoy recovered it! It was just what the Raiders needed to turn the game around. But the officials waved the play off. They ruled that Lytle was stopped before the **fumble**. They gave the ball back to the Broncos, who scored on the next play.

The Raiders never recovered. The Broncos advanced to the Super Bowl. Replays clearly showed Lytle fumbled the ball.

IT IS REMEMBERED AS ONE OF THE BIGGEST BLOWN CALLS IN FOOTBALL HISTORY.

CHAPTER 1

REFEREE RESPONSIBILITIES

Every NFL game has seven officials on the field. The head official is the referee. The referee oversees the other officials and announces all penalties. The other officials are the back judge, side judge, field judge, line judge, down judge, and umpire.

Each official has specific responsibilities during every play. They cover a certain part of the field. You can see their positions on the back of their jerseys.

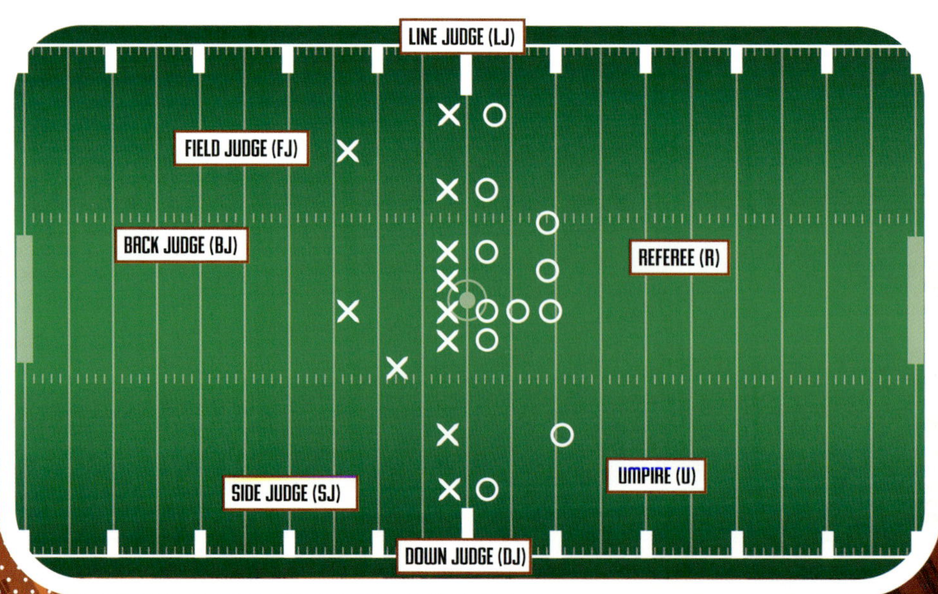

There are more than 100 different penalties that can be called in an NFL game. An NFL field is 360 feet long and 160 feet wide. There are 22 players on the field. That is a lot to cover for the officials. If an official misses a single penalty call, it can change the outcome of the game. That is a lot of pressure.

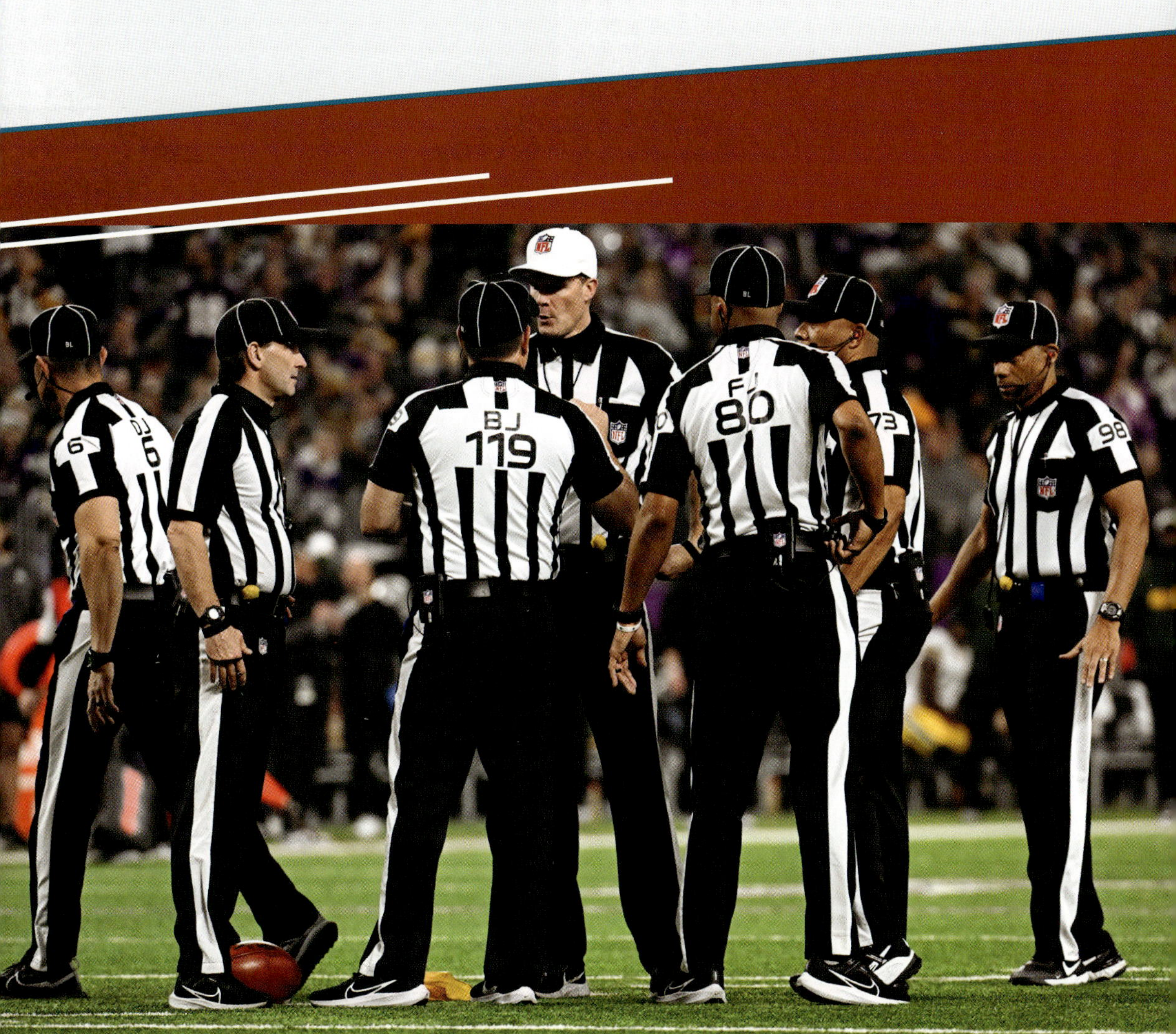

Getting the chance to be on the field with the greatest football players takes lots of hard work. There are only 121 on-field officials in the NFL.

IT CAN TAKE TEN OR MORE YEARS TO EVEN HAVE THE CHANCE TO MAKE IT TO THE NFL.

Clete Blakeman is a great example of the dedication it takes to make it to the top. Blakeman has been an NFL official since 2008 and a referee since 2010. His journey began by coaching high school football with his dad. Then he moved up to small college programs. Blakeman worked hard and landed a spot as an official for Division I college football. Still, the NFL was his dream. Blakeman traveled overseas, working as an official for NFL Europe for three seasons before getting his shot in the NFL.

TIME OUT

Do you ever play *Madden Football*? The voice you hear as the referee is Clete Blakeman.

In addition to the seven on-field officials, each NFL game has officials who work in the booth. Their job is to help see things the on-field officials might miss. That includes penalties, injuries, and clock management. They also review every scoring play and turnover to confirm it with the on-field officials.

In New York City, another group of officials monitor every game to make the calls when a play is challenged. These officials are the final decision-makers when a coach throws a red challenge flag. Even with so many officials watching every player on every play, calls still get missed.

LET'S LOOK AT SOME OF THE BIGGEST MISSED CALLS IN NFL HISTORY.

CHAPTER 2

THE MUSIC CITY MIRACLE

The visiting Buffalo Bills had just driven the length of the field and kicked the go-ahead field goal. It was the 1999 AFC Wild Card Game. With just 16 seconds left on the clock, the home team now trailed 16–15. It would take a miracle for the Tennessee Titans to come back and win the game.

Bills kicker Steve Christie launched a high, short kick. Fullback Lorenzo Neal caught the kick. He quickly handed the ball off to tight end Frank Wycheck. As the Bills defense chased Wycheck to the right, he spun and threw the ball across the field. Kevin Dyson caught the pass—and raced 75 yards for the game-winning touchdown! But not so fast . . .

TIME OUT

The winning play was called the "Home Run Throwback." The Titans had practiced it every week all season, waiting for the perfect time to try it in a game.

The Bills believed Wycheck's pass was a forward pass. Forward passes aren't allowed on kickoff returns. You can only throw backward or to the side. From the replays shown during the game, it was hard to tell if the pass was thrown forward.

The officials took time and reviewed the play. If the pass had been thrown forward, the touchdown would not count. However, the officials ruled it was a **lateral** pass.

IT WAS A TOUCHDOWN FOR THE TITANS!

The Titans won the game 22–16. Referee Phil Luckett, who made the call, says it was the right one.

“There was no evidence that it was forward,” Luckett said in an interview with NFL Films. “It looked straight across or maybe very slightly backwards.”

The NFL defended the officials, insisting they got the call right. They even hired a computer **analyst** to examine the footage of the play. The analyst issued a ruling saying the pass was a legal, lateral pass.

The big play saved the Titans' season. The team advanced to the Super Bowl. For the Buffalo Bills, the last-second loss was the beginning of a record-setting run of losing. For the next 17 seasons, the Bills missed the playoffs. It was the longest streak for any team in the Super Bowl era.

TIME OUT

Nashville, Tennessee, is known as "Music City" because of its country music scene. The Titans' winning play is known as the "Music City Miracle" because their home field is in Nashville.

You've taken the place of referee Phil Luckett on the field.

The Bills kick the ball. You see Lorenzo Neal catch and hand it to Frank Wycheck.

Wycheck throws the ball across the field to Kevin Dyson, who races 75 yards for the touchdown.

Did Wycheck throw a forward pass?

Does the touchdown stand?

CHAPTER 3

SUPER BOWL STOLEN

It was January 20, 2019. The New Orleans Saints were hosting the Los Angeles Rams for the National Football Conference (NFC) Championship. With the game tied at 20, the Saints were in field goal range. Quarterback Drew Brees threw a pass to Tommylee Lewis.

Rams cornerback Nickell Robey-Coleman drilled Lewis with a helmet-to-helmet hit. It looked like an easy pass **interference** call. The Saints should get a first down. Then they could run down the clock and kick the game-winning field goal.

SO WHERE IS THE CONTROVERSY?

The officials never threw a flag! Even if the officials threw the flag, it wasn't a guarantee the Saints would win. They could have fumbled the ball on a bad snap. The Saints kicker could have missed the kick. The Rams could have blocked the field goal. But they never even got the chance!

TIME OUT

The common nickname for this game is the "NOLA No-Call."

Sean Payton, the Saints' head coach, couldn't believe it! Neither could the fans, the players, or the millions of viewers. The game went into overtime, and the Rams won 26–23.

After the game, Robey-Coleman admitted he had committed the penalty. "I got there too early. I was beat, and I was trying to save the touchdown."

Even NFL **Commissioner** Roger Goodell agreed that the refs blew the call on the field. This is what he said during a press conference for Super Bowl LIII. "Our officials are human. And they're not going to get it right every time."

Months after the mistake, the NFL changed the rules. For one season, coaches were allowed to throw a challenge flag to review pass interference calls (or non-calls).

However, the rule change wasn't very successful. In the 2019 season, coaches challenged pass interference 81 times. Only 13 calls were reversed. This showed that officials get it right most of the time.

TIME OUT

Two Saints fans sued the NFL to try to force them to replay the end of the game. They lost the lawsuit.

You are the closest official to the play. It happened so fast.

You hear the hit, but did you see it clearly? If you did, was it an illegal helmet-to-helmet hit?

Also, did Nickell Robey-Coleman hit Tommylee Lewis early? If so, was it pass interference?

CHAPTER 4

THE FAIL MARY

The 2012 NFL season began with replacement officials. And it fell apart in week three on *Monday Night Football*. The Green Bay Packers were visiting the Seattle Seahawks. Seattle was trailing 12–7 with time running out. Seattle had one last play—the **Hail Mary**. Rookie quarterback Russell Wilson launched a high, arching bomb into the end zone.

Receiver Golden Tate was ready. So was Packers defender M.D. Jennings. Both players grabbed the ball on the way to the ground. Two officials were standing next to each other in the end zone. One official signaled touchdown. The other official signaled interception.

WAS IT A TOUCHDOWN OR AN INTERCEPTION?

TIME OUT

The NFL and the regular officials were arguing over a new contract because the officials wanted more money. The NFL chose to lock them out and use replacement officials.

The play was automatically reviewed. The officials called "**simultaneous** possession." By rule, that made it a Seattle touchdown. The Seahawks won the game 14–12.

The refs made multiple mistakes. First, Golden Tate pushed off the defender before the ball arrived. This is offensive pass interference. It would have ended the game and given the Packers the win.

Then there is the call of simultaneous possession. Replays show Packers defender M.D. Jennings catching the ball. Tate is just grabbing at it as Jennings has control. Again, this would give the Packers the win.

However, the biggest mistake appeared to be the NFL's decision to use replacement officials. What made it worse was that it happened on *Monday Night Football*. More than 16 million fans tuned in to see the game and the bad call. Following the Monday night disaster, the fans were upset. The players felt cheated. The media was angry. And the NFL admitted they got it wrong.

TIME OUT

Just two days after the Monday night game, the NFL announced a deal with the officials had been reached.

You've taken the place of one of the officials in the end zone.

Russell Wilson launches the ball into the end zone. Seattle receiver Golden Tate jumps up to grab it. Green Bay defender M.D. Jennings jumps to grab it too.

Both players have their hands on the ball. Simultaneous possession is one of the toughest calls to make.

Was it a touchdown or an interception?

The work of NFL officials has changed a lot since that game in 1978 between the Raiders and Broncos. The speed of the game is faster. The hits are harder. The offenses run more complicated plays. The use of instant replay helps. But it doesn't fix every problem. The job of the NFL officials is one of the hardest in pro sports.

Do you think you have what it takes to be an NFL official someday?

GLOSSARY

analyst (AN-uh-list)—someone who studies data and reports the findings

commissioner (kuh-MISH-uh-ner)—a person in charge of a department

fumble (FUHM-buhl)—to lose control of the ball

Hail Mary (HAYL MEH-ree)—a long, forward pass in football where completion is unlikely; usually happens at the end of a game

interference (in-ter-FEER-uhns)—getting in the way or creating difficulties for someone

lateral (LAT-er-uhl)—to the side

rookie (ROOH-kee)—first-year player in a professional sports league

simultaneous (sih-muhl-TAY-nee-uhs)—at the same time

READ MORE

Chandler, Matt. *Lamar Jackson: Superstar Quarterback*. North Mankato, MN: Capstone, 2021.

Halprin, David. *Football Biographies for Kids: The Greatest NFL Players from the 1960s to Today*. New York: Callisto Kids, 2022.

Mann, Dionna L. *Tom Brady vs. Peyton Manning: Football Legends Face Off*. North Mankato, MN: Capstone, 2024.

INTERNET SITES

NFL Football Operations: Becoming an Official
operations.nfl.com/officiating/the-officials/officiating-development/becoming-an-official

Pro Football Hall of Fame: Teams
profootballhof.com/teams

Sports Illustrated Kids: Football
sikids.com/football

INDEX

ABOUT THE AUTHOR

Matt Chandler is the author of more than 90 books for children and thousands of articles published in newspapers and magazines. He writes mostly nonfiction books with a focus on sports, ghosts and haunted places, and graphic novels. Matt lives in New York.